21st **Century Skills INNOVATION LIBRARY**

MAKERS As Innovators

More Web Design with HTML5

CHERRY LAKE PUBLISHING • ANN ARBOR, MICHIGAN

by Colleen van Lent

A Note to Adults: Please review the instructions for the activities in this book before allowing children to do them. Be sure to help them with any activities you do not think they can safely complete on their own.

A Note to Kids: Be sure to ask an adult for help with these activities when you need it. Always put your safety first!

Published in the United States of America by Cherry Lake Publishing
Ann Arbor, Michigan
www.cherrylakepublishing.com

Series editor: Kristin Fontichiaro

Photo Credits: Cover and page 1, The Design Lab; pages 5, 14, 21, and 22, Colleen van Lent; page 8, Waag Society / tinyurl.com/lfyyrpw / CC-BY-2.0.

Library of Congress Cataloging-in-Publication Data
van Lent, Colleen. More web design with
  HTML5 / by Colleen Van Lent.
    pages cm — (21st century skills innovation library)
  Audience: Grades 4 to 6.
  Includes bibliographical references and index.
  ISBN 978-1-63188-868-7 (lib. bdg.) — ISBN 978-1-63188-892-2 (pdf) — ISBN 978-1-63188-880-9 (pbk.) —ISBN 978-1-63188-904-2 (e-book)
  1. HTML (Document markup language)—Juvenile literature.
2. Internet programming—Juvenile literature. 3. Web sites—Juvenile literature.
I. Title.
  QA76.76.H94V359 2015
  006.74—dc23   2014024985

Cherry Lake Publishing would like to acknowledge the work of The Partnership for 21st Century Skills. Please visit *www.p21.org* for more information.

Printed in the United States of America
Corporate Graphics Inc.
January 2015

Contents

Chapter 1

Creating a Better Web Page

So you've built your first Web page and posted it online. It works, but it is very basic, and you would like to improve it. You have learned about different kinds of tags and their **syntax**, but you suspect that there is more to learn about Web design. You're right! The next step is to learn good design practice.

To accomplish this, we are going to create a navigation bar. Navigation bars are a common way to link a series of pages together on a Web site. Sometimes they are located along the top of a site. Other times, they are along the side. However, they all have the same purpose: to help people find information on your site.

A good navigation bar is *styled*, *accessible*, *fluid*, and *interactive*. But what do these terms mean?

Web pages almost always have a navigation bar across the top of the page (as shown here) or down the left side. They help readers quickly find the information they are looking for.

Styled

Proper styling is handled using cascading style sheets (CSS). When using CSS, you don't need to style each individual tag of your page. Instead, you can write rules that apply to the whole page. In this book, you will learn the first steps of styling pages with CSS.

Accessible

The code for your navigation bar will use something called semantic tags. These tags rarely change the appearance of your page. Instead, semantic tags provide special information to **assistive devices** that people may be using to view your page. This makes your pages accessible to people who are blind or otherwise disabled. Semantic tags are easy to include, and they are helpful to many people. As a result, it is good to get in the habit of using them.

Fluid

People will use many different devices to view your page once it is published online. Some people use desktop or laptop computers, while others use tablets or smartphones. The screens of these devices have very different shapes and sizes. This causes pages to look different on different devices. Fluid design is the process of making sure your pages will look good on as many different devices as possible. The **content** stays the same regardless of the device. However, the way the content is arranged on the page may change depending on the type of device or screen size.

Interactive

Once you have your page looking the way you want, you can start to make it more interactive. For example, we can make it so the navigation bar will change based on the user's mouse movement.

These four concepts can be applied to any portion of a Web page, not just a navigation bar. However, a navigation bar is a great place to practice adding interactivity to your web page. You can work your way up to more complicated interactivity as you get more comfortable with HTML.

Internet Safety

Remember to get your parents' permission before posting a Web page online. You should never publish personal information about yourself, such as your full name, home address, school name, or phone number. There is no easy way to include privacy settings on the Web pages you make. Once you post a Web page online, it is easy for anyone to find. Be selective about the pictures you post, too. You never know who will be looking at your page. Finally, do not put your e-mail address on your site. Web crawlers are programs that search the Web to gather information from sites. If one of them finds your e-mail address, you will probably start to receive a lot of spam messages.

This book assumes that you know the basic structure of a Web page and how to create and save files. It is okay if there are some tags (snippets of code) that you don't know. You can always look them up. The most important thing is to understand that you will make mistakes along the way. Running into problems as you write HTML code is normal, even for pros! Many of the problems you face will be caused by simple typos. Just be patient. In the end, you will have a great-looking site!

You may not write all of your code perfectly on the first try. Keep testing your code, and if you need help, ask!

Chapter 2

Navigation Bars

You probably learned the basics of HTML by creating a single Web page. But now that you are learning more advanced HTML skills, it's time to make a multipage Web site! When your site has multiple pages, you need to make it easy for users to see everything you have created. This is where the navigation bar comes in. Navigation bars are a way for people to explore your site without using the forward and back buttons in their Web browsers. They also organize the many pages of your site into sections. Follow the steps below to start building a multipage site with a navigation bar.

Step One: Plan

Decide how many pages your site will have and what you will name them. You can always add more pages or take some away. However, you should decide on good file names right away. We will have four pages in our example: a home page, a page about sports, a page about dance, and a page about our favorite foods. Their file names are index.html, sports.html, dance.html, and food.html. Avoid naming your pages things like page1.html or page2.html—it will get confusing. Use descriptive names instead!

Step Two: Create

Create an .html file for each of your pages. Don't worry about the content yet, but make sure you put an <h1> header tag in each page to show the main content. For example, use <h1>Favorite Restaurants</h1> in the food.html page and <h1>Dance</h1> in the dance page. Don't forget to include ".html" in the file names.

Naming Conventions

Do you know why the main page of a Web site is typically named index.html? The ".html" part is needed because computers know that files ending in ".html" are Web pages. This is what tells the computer to open the file in a browser such as Chrome, Safari, or Firefox. The "index" part of the file name is a **convention**. A convention is not a strict rule. Rather, it is something that Web designers have agreed on to better understand each other's code. If you are looking at a page called index.html, you can safely assume that it is the main page of its site.

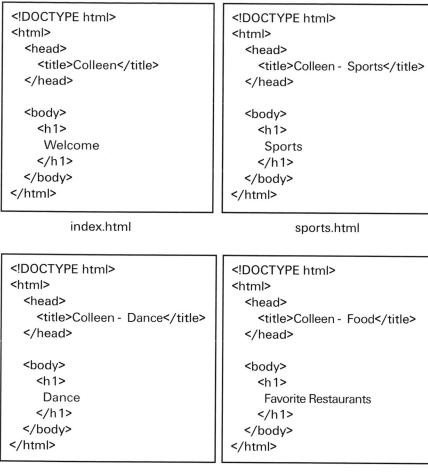

```
<!DOCTYPE html>
<html>
  <head>
    <title>Colleen</title>
  </head>

  <body>
    <h1>
      Welcome
    </h1>
  </body>
</html>
```

index.html

```
<!DOCTYPE html>
<html>
  <head>
    <title>Colleen - Sports</title>
  </head>

  <body>
    <h1>
      Sports
    </h1>
  </body>
</html>
```

sports.html

```
<!DOCTYPE html>
<html>
  <head>
    <title>Colleen - Dance</title>
  </head>

  <body>
    <h1>
      Dance
    </h1>
  </body>
</html>
```

dance.html

```
<!DOCTYPE html>
<html>
  <head>
    <title>Colleen - Food</title>
  </head>

  <body>
    <h1>
      Favorite Restaurants
    </h1>
  </body>
</html>
```

food.html

Step Three: Tag and Link

One of the semantic tags in HTML is <nav>. It doesn't provide any special styling. Instead, it tells the computer where you are going to put links between the pages of your site. This is especially important for accessibility. For instance, it helps people using screen readers to identify the important topics of the site right away. And anyone who is restricted to using the tab button instead of a mouse to navigate your site can skip other links and head straight to the important ones.

The code below shows a <nav> tag enclosing four links—one for each of your pages. If you named your files something different than the example, make your code match your file names. Remember that consistent spelling and capitalization are very important.

Where does this code belong in your file? Technically, you could put this code anywhere. However, most people expect the navigation bar to be near the top of the page. As a result, it is usually a good idea to put it in a <header> tag along with any <h1> tags.

```
<nav>
   <a href = "index.html">Home page</a>
   <a href = "sports.html">Sports</a>
   <a href = "dance.html">Dance</a>
   <a href = "food.html">Favorite Restaurants</a>
</nav>
```

When you write code, it is important to make small changes and test your work often. Write code, then test, then fix the code, then test, and repeat until everything is just right. As you are working on the navigation bar, place it only in the index.html file at first.

It may be tempting to put the navigation bar code into all of your pages right from the start. But this is not a good idea. Almost no one writes perfect code the first time, even pros. Instead, you will probably discover that you have a few bugs in your code as you go. Instead of trying to fix those bugs in multiple files, you can copy and paste the finished code from the index file into the other files.

```html
<!DOCTYPE html>
<html>
  <head>
   <title>Colleen</title>
  </head>

  <body>
   <header>
    <h1>Welcome</h1>
    <nav>
        <a href = "index.html">Home Page</a>
        <a href = "sports.html">Sports</a>
        <a href = "dance.html">Dance</a>
        <a href = "food.html">Favorite Restaurants</a>
    </nav>
   </header>
  </body>
</html>
```

Here is what the nav code looks like when it is placed inside the code for the entire page.

Step Four: Test

Once you have typed in the code for your navigation bar, it is time to make sure it works correctly. To test the links, begin by clicking on the first one. In our example, this would be the home page. More than likely, it will look like nothing happened when you click on this link. This is because the "new" page is the one we were already looking at.

Now click on the next link. If it doesn't work, there are two likely reasons. Either you haven't placed your .html files in the same folder or you made a typo in

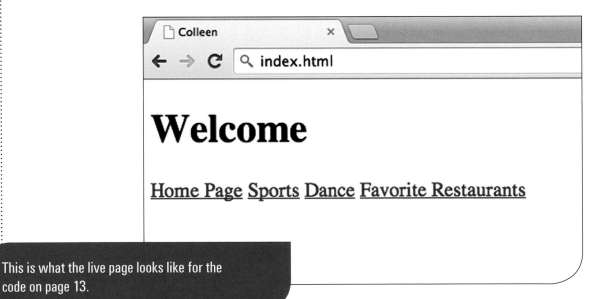

This is what the live page looks like for the code on page 13.

your code. Make sure that the file in the link matches the file name exactly. For example, some browsers don't consider "Sports.html" to be the same thing as "sports.html".

If the link was successful, use the back button in your browser to go back to the home page. Check the other links in the same way. Once you're sure that everything is working, you can get to work improving your navigation bar's style!

Chapter 3

Styling Like a Pro

I n your previous HTML files, you may have used style attributes to add cool background colors or adjust the position of an image. For instance, to add background color to a paragraph using attributes, you would type the following:

```
<p style= "backgound-color: #CCFFCC">
```

This is called inline styling. It is a simple way to make a quick change to the appearance of your page. Inline styling is great for beginners. However, a method called internal styling is much more useful once you get comfortable with HTML. Internal styling lets you write rules that apply to all the uses of a particular tag, rather than styling the elements of your pages one at a time.

Imagine that you have a site with 5, 10, or even 100 pages. You want to use blue as the font color for all of your paragraphs. Later, you decide you want to change it to red. It would be annoying, time-consuming, and error-prone to go in and change all of the tags one by one on every page. Internal styling rules make the process much simpler. A rule is coded like this:

```
selector {
        property: value;
}
```

The *selector* is the tag you want the rule to affect. The curly bracket after the tag name starts your rule. The *property* is the attribute you want to change, and the *value* is how you want that property to be styled. The second curly bracket ends the rule. It is possible to put as many "property: value" pairs as you want inside a single rule, as long as they are separated by semicolons.

Suppose that we want to style the header of our pages to give it a nice green background color. The code could be:

```
header {
        background: #CCFFCC;
}
```

Defining Colors

There are four common ways to define colors:

- color names
- hexadecimal values
- RGB values
- RGBA values

Color names are simply the full names of colors, spelled out. For example, you would type "red" or "green." Hexadecimal values are what we use for most of the examples in this book. These are special codes that each represent a specific color. For example, the hexadecimal value #CCFFCC displays a light green color.

RGB stands for "red," "green," and "blue." RGB colors are created by blending different amounts of those three colors. Higher numbers mean more of a color. RGBA values are the same as RGB, but they also include a value for "alpha-transparency." This just means you can fade the color. A low number in the fourth position makes it lighter. A high number makes it darker.

It is fine to use color names when you are first learning to code. However, it is better to use one of the other methods once you are ready to publish. RGB and hexadecimal values give you far more colors to choose from. Using them also ensures that your page will look the same regardless of which browser or device the page is viewed on.

```
header {
        background: #CCFFCC;
}
```

red value   green value   blue value

```
header {
        background: rgb (0, 0, 255);
}
```

transparency

```
header {
        background: rgb (0, 255, .75);
}
```

What if we wanted to style the navigation bar to make it pop out a bit from the rest of the header? We could use this code to give it a white background and include a solid black border that is 3 **pixels** wide. The border property uses multiple values:

- the width (in pixels) of the line
- the style (solid, dashed, dotted, etc.) of the line
- the color of the line

```
nav {
        background: #0000FF;
        border: 3px solid #00CC00;
}
```

As long as you are careful to place curly brackets and semicolons in the right places, writing style rules should be easy. The only question left is where in your code to put the rules. Because you don't want the rules to show up on the page itself, add them to the <head> section. The <head> tag holds a page's metadata. This is information that helps the browser display a page but does not actually show up on a viewer's screen. Right now, your <head> tag only has the title information for your page. It is time to change that.

Open your index.html file and add the <style> and </style> tags after the <title> tag. The style *attribute* applies special properties to a single tag. However, the style *tag* will apply all of the rules inside it to the entire page.

Did it work? If not, try adding just one rule at a time. Sometimes you might need to refresh the page in your browser for the changes to take effect. Once you get it to work, try adding additional properties, such as *text-align*, *color*, or *font-style*.

```
<head>
   <title> Colleen</title>

   <style>
   header{
      background:#0000FF;
      text-align: center;
   }
   nav{
      background: #FFFFFF;
      border: 5px solid #000000;
   }
   </style>
</head>
```

Adding style rules to your header is an easy way to change the look of an entire page.

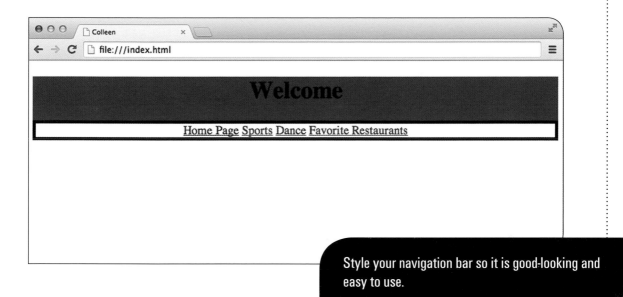

Style your navigation bar so it is good-looking and easy to use.

Styling the Links

While the page now looks slightly prettier, you haven't yet seen the advantages of using the <style> tag instead of the style attribute. That is because there is only one <header> and <nav> in the page. It will be easier to see the benefits once you style the links in your navigation bar.

Before you code, you should decide how you want the links to look. Proper spacing and accessible colors are key to good navigation. Have you ever visited a Web site where the links are all squished together? What about pages where you need to scroll over to see all of the links? If the links are too close, it can be difficult to click on the right one. This is especially true if you are using a mobile device. If links are too far apart, people may not even see them. And don't forget about pages where the links are impossible to read because there is no **contrast** between font colors and background colors.

Use the margin and padding properties to modify the spacing of your links. The margin is the amount of blank space the browser will include around an element. Padding is the blank space within the element.

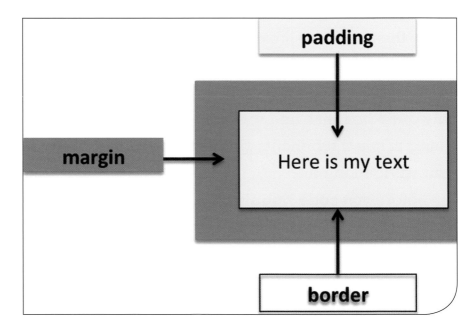

Sometimes the difference between these two is vague. Adding a border can make it easier to distinguish between them.

Spacing is important for more than just the navigation bar. Most container elements (such as <body>, <header>, <nav>, and <p>) look better with a little bit of margin space, padding, or both. If you think your text is too close to the edge of something else, add a little extra spacing.

The Rules

We only want to style the links in our navigation bar, rather than all of the links in the page. If you wanted to style all of the links, you would just use "a" as the selector in the rule. Instead, we want to style only those <a> tags that are inside the <nav> tag. The following rule puts a 10 percent margin around all link elements that are inside a <nav> tag.

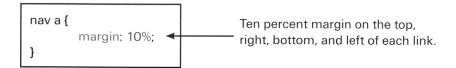

```
nav a {
        margin: 10%;
}
```

Ten percent margin on the top, right, bottom, and left of each link.

Using percentages instead of specific numbers of pixels will help make your design fluid. When using percentages, the actual width of the margin will shrink and grow to fit a user's screen. Pixels are a perfectly good way to measure fonts and borders. These elements will usually look good regardless of the screen size. But when it comes to padding and margins, always stick to percentages. A 150-pixel margin might look great on your laptop, but it would probably be far too large for a mobile phone.

Some property names can have variations. For instance, in the case of margin and padding properties, you might specify one value to use on all four sides, as we did on page 23. However, you can also choose to specify different values for each of the four sides.

```
a {
      margin-left: 10%;
      margin-top: 2%;
}
```

Ten percent margin on the left of each link, a 2% margin on top, and no margin on the right or bottom.

Putting It Together

Browsers will automatically change the color of your links when they are clicked on. However, you can choose to set these colors yourself. Always think about color combinations that will look good and be easy to read.

Here are two more properties that will help with your navigation bar.

- border-radius: This is a numerical value that rounds the edges of the padding. A small number creates a slight curve, while bigger numbers will make your links appear to be very rounded. This only works if you have a background color.

- text-decoration: This removes the underline that browsers place under links. It will give your navigation bar a cleaner, simpler look. Don't overuse this property, though. You want people to know what is a link and what isn't.

Adding this last bit of code may cause a problem for you. If your links have too much padding, they may sneak out of the boundaries of the <nav> tag. Not a problem. Just add some padding to the <nav> tag itself. Remember: code, test, code, test . . . success!

```
nav a {
    background: #0000FF;
    color: #FFFFFF;
    margin: 5%;
    padding: 1%;
    border-radius: 10%;
    text-decoration: none;
}
```

Interaction: The Hover Pseudo-Class

The last thing we will do is add an interactive component to your navigation bar. Did you ever notice that your cursor changes from an arrow to a pointer when you mouse over a link in your browser? You can add your own special mouse-over animation by using a pseudo-class. A rule with a pseudo-class looks for special circumstances and only applies the styling temporarily. One common pseudo-class is hover. Simply add the pseudo-class after the selector in your rule. Make sure to include a colon between the selector and the pseudo-class. Do not use spaces.

This rule tells browsers to change the background color and font color of a link any time the mouse

```
nav a:hover {
    background: #FFFFFF;
    color: #000000;
}
```

hovers above it. When the mouse moves away from the link, the colors go back to what they were before. Changing the colors is just one of the many options you can play with. Try changing the font size, padding, color transparency, or border radius using pseudo-classes. But remember that while such visual tricks are very cool, including too many can leave you with a page that is hard to navigate.

Once your navigation bar is just the way you want it, you can copy and paste the code from the <head> section of your index.html file into all of your other files. Easy, right? Now you can see the benefits of using internal styling!

Chapter 4

Finishing Touches

Hopefully your site is functional and the navigation bar looks great. If something isn't working right, make sure that you used all of the necessary semicolons and curly brackets in your code. If you forget one, the browser will ignore all of the rules that come after it in your code.

Now it is time to make the rest of your page look good. As you add new content and tags, you will create additional style rules for your paragraphs, headings, and other elements. Make sure to test your page every time you add something to the code!

Moving from inline styling (the style attribute) to internal styling (using the style tag) is a big step toward becoming a better Web designer. Internal styling cuts down on the time it takes to update your pages. It also gives a consistent look to your site. If you are interested in learning more about CSS, you can look online for tips. For example, you could learn how to create a single page of rules that can be used to control the look of any number of other pages. Search the Web for information about "CSS3 external style sheets" to get started. Good luck!

The <details> Tag

The <details> tag is a new tag to HTML5. It allows users to hide and show some of your page's content on demand. Like an HTML-coded list, it has two parts: a summary and a description. The summary is always visible. It has an icon displayed next to it. The description can be opened and closed by clicking on the icon.

The code:

```
<details>
    <summary>Brief summary goes here... </summary>
    Longer description goes here...
</details>
```

When it is closed:

▶ Brief summary goes here...

When it is open:

▼ Brief summary goes here...
Longer description goes here...

Because the <details> tag is a new part of HTML, not all browsers support it yet. If someone is looking at your page with Firefox or Internet Explorer, for example, the summary will always be visible. No icon will appear. Keep this in mind if you decide to include

Glossary

assistive devices (uh-SIS-tiv di-VISE-iz) software or hardware that helps disabled people use computers

content (KAHN-tent) text, photos, videos, and other things posted on a Web page

contrast (KAHN-trast) a difference between things that makes them stand apart from one another

convention (kuhn-VEN-shuhn) a customary or accepted way to behave or do something

pixels (PIKS-uhlz) the tiny dots on a video screen or computer monitor that make up the visual image

syntax (SIN-taks) the rules that govern a programming or command language and determine the way that letters, numbers, and symbols must be entered

Find Out More

BOOKS

van Lent, Colleen. *Web Design with HTML5*. Ann Arbor, MI: Cherry Lake Publishing, 2014.

Poolos, Jamie. *Designing, Building, and Maintaining Web Sites.* New York: Rosen Central, 2011.

WEB SITES

Codeacademy

www.codeacademy.com
Follow self-paced tutorials for learning HTML and other programming languages.

Mozilla Webmaker

https://webmaker.org
Mozilla, the nonprofit organization behind the Firefox browser, will teach you strategies for viewing source code and coding your own pages.

Index

About the Author

Colleen van Lent is a computer scientist who teaches at the University of Michigan School of Information in Ann Arbor.